Al Bean's Poetry Dream

Alice Taylor

BookLeaf Publishing
India | USA | UK

Presentation by *BookLeaf Publishing*

Web: www.bookleafpub.com

E-mail: info@bookleafpub.com

ISBN: 978-93-5744-331-9

First edition 2022

1

Start at the beginning:
Green lights
Fist fights
Feel it run up and down my back
Bites
Looking for the world
As a child
Defiled
Ridiculed and exiled
A world of her creation
'Such a wild imagination!'
'She's meant to write'
Misheard it, right
The wrongs of those who made her
Save her
Giver, give her
Lungs filled with the spirits of the river
Spirits stick with her
Bones
Float underwater
Salty daughter

2

The sleepless men
Are by your side again.
I've seen them, darkened brow and folded hands
Standing tall, as quiet as they can
Sentinels.

Earth bound
Not even the smallest sound,
I've watched them, slow in their approach
They don't chase, and they won't coax
Steady.

Frozen
Will their eyes to open
You're already planning your escape
Inside, you know that it's too late
Keeper.

3

There were creatures in that house
I leapt from windows
Cars
Feelings
I can't hear the screaming.
All that I recall
Are feet smashing the pavement
Chest on fire
Cold air
Slap across the face
I'd run, I'd run
I'd run until I found the place.
You know you're close when you feel on your
ankles
Dancing, tickling blades
Welcoming you home.
It's been a long night, sit down,
wait.
Those the eyes I came to ssee.
Humble, gentle, brown

Pressing your face against my own
And I am safe.
Until, I returned one day
And all of you had left
For the shelves
Of the shop.

4

Dancing along
But
Not
Quite
In
The right timing
Push or pull?
Each movement
Has me asking
It looks oh so small
Each action
Casts out circles
Do they move beyond what our eyes see?
Do they push, pull further?
Do they rise as steam?
Its dance moves
Compliment
Those steady steps:
Entrechat
Fly on warmth
Hot feet
Dance away, dance away.

5

Along the old streets
A song troughs and peaks
Wind whistles it into his ears

It whirrs for a while
Travels on to his smile
Plays its footprints and stamps on his fear

Oh wouldn't you know,
Tucked away from the snow
Is a place that will take it away

Where the music will flutter
Neon lights through a shutter
Make a fond eve of your day

Though he tries to deny
That song spins in his mind
His feet march their way in through the door

Songstress shadows, they snake
Strike him hard, lonely rake
Joins the fabric of cold, stony floor

Nobody will know
Where those lonely men go
Nobody will tell you her name

But do a girl wrong
And the sound of that song
Will freeze you, will drive you
Insane

6

Always the same thing I do
I'm more invested than you
Spend my time like
Money that isn't mine
It's all fiction, my prediction
Is that I will hide away
With my stories, take the pain
Guess that I was never taught
Not to fall for my own thoughts

The weather is always better
In my imagination, thinking of us together
These pictures I paint aren't real but
That doesn't mean I don't feel this
Oh to overthink
Further down I sink
At least things look prettier
Under the water

It's not that you made a mistake
My heart just gets carried away, leading me on again
You'd think I'd have learned, but I'm stupid
For you, say jump and I'll do it
Drown myself in my own stories
Let me go, let me float away
I prefer it this way

7

She's got desert glass eyes
She crashed down in the forest
Storms in her words
And a spell on her tongue
She's on the run
Dirt on her arms and dust on her face
Bloodied up cheek
We'd better brace ourselves

He's got a shard in his soul
Never thought one could get it so cold
Shivering mess
His cries are rousing
Left in a state of undress
Slumbering cracks of the earth
His breath is clouded
Sorry words eke out
Blood on the snow

8

I used to get in trouble
For trying to smuggle
Shannon tinnies from the fridge.
Warm days and a warm place
Each face
Smiling, 'nice to see ya'
Give it a few years and that birdlike chatter
Would bring on the worst of headaches.

This used to be the good place
The one place
Quirks and drifters felt safe
But now

It's all just dirty laundry
That you've muddied yourself
Talking such a good talk
When your own home is filthy.

This place has gone from warm
Safe, secure
To drugs, to lies, dishonesty.
I know I shouldn't talk about it
Better just to walk from it

But it hurts to see a castle fall to ruin
Because of someone else's lying.

It hurts that the backdrop to those formative, drunken years
Has changed and yet its not
The bricks and bar all look the same
The soul has gone to rot.
It wouldn't surprise me if the spirits there had fled
There's only so much room for the dead.

It's your choice if that's how you'd like to live
But I would rather leave.

9

Fingernails against the palm of my hand
There are eyes in everything I see
Why won't anybody listen to me?
Have I turned invisible,
Or do you just want me to be?

There are demons hiding under my skin
They protect me from reality
We're friends now
Somewhat codependently.

I'm in trouble again
Each tiny little fragment is lodging itself in my
brain
One by one
Try to keep myself together
I can feel the fractures
Where the light comes out
Blinding this.

I can't breathe again, I'm losing
Control
This isn't my choosing
My breathing gets faster

But I don't want the air
My heartbeat is racing
But I'm still as her laughter.

Someone else has a place in my mind
And it hurts too much
Can anybody see me?
I'm sure I'm still here.

There's that monster I don't recognise
She hides in mirrors
Smoke
And corners
If I promise I'll be good
Will you pull my body out?

I'm sinking but I've drowned before
The taste on my tongue's not a new one
I'm getting bored
I've felt the tide pulling me under
The cold has known me, and cradled me as I spin
There's the green light again
Escaping
The sea is swallowing me whole.

10

They were sent from a planet far away
They're speaking in different voices
I think we heard it once
But it went back to another frequency
I can't find the channel again
So I'm jumping timelines
Watching the waves
Laugh at the thought of this
Strange little world as the stone
Stand back,
Count the waves
And dance between them
Taking comfort in the fact they look so similar
But
Slightly differ
Codeword, codeword
Codeword Taylor
Take that word
Dear lord and saviour
Spread throughout the different paths
Confused masses, aftermath
Will they learn, or will they flounder?
With so much choice,
It doesn't matter.

11

Crash and burn
They laugh and tie me to the carseat, blindfold, smothered
I've no idea
Of what they're after
Hence the torture
Locked behind the wheel with my foot pressed harder
I wanna
Throw myself against the tarmac
Just a little pause to get myself back
If I have to die
Just to keep that part alive
Is it so bad?
Their matches
Keep catching
The lick of a nearby breeze
Strung up on the pyre but I don't feel anything
I want to scream
But all I hear is birdsong
Isn't even me they want
Just entertainment
Puppet of my own, insane
Imagination

12

I feel a calm in my heart
I know I will love you until the day I die
Rock n roll and quiet corners
Stars and smokes
The purest thing I know.

Wind in my hair in your car
The space we knew best
The air whipped my face
My soul was at rest
When I was with you.

Called me up,
Roadside panic attacks
You wouldn't do that
To just anyone?
I knew then our days were numbered.

Seeing that pain in your eyes
I knew you'd fucked up
But you're only a man
Old enough to paint a picture
Daddy Issues
There for you
Time to drive that car into a wall

I had to burn it all.
The thing that I loved most
I knew that it must die
If I was to save your mind
At every chance I could I played
The song of wild hysterics
And I mastered it.

I miss you every day
But part of love
Is knowing when to tear it down
And walk away.

13

Train tracks and bus stops
Thistles and raindrops
Grey skies shine on me but only when I'm alone.

I didn't lose a part of myself,
Just pressed
pause.

Late nights in cars, streetlights, heavy leaves on rooves.
Everything when I'm in the only one,
Invisible when she's in the room.

The only person's secret I will be is my own
The only bed I'm curled up in is
home
We're all still far from figuring it out but
The further you are
The closer I feel.

14

The moon is lower than I am.
The moon is so low, I think that it could fall for you.
The moon is so low, I could touch it
I sliced to sky to leave a slick of red
Bleeding over all your heads
I'll tear a hole in the sky so you can keep howling.

15

Sometimes I want to swim in the river
Sometimes I want to drown
Be careful if you join me
It may drag you down
Or you could float forever
Smiles spread across your lips
The water's warm beneath you
Until that smile slips.

16

Oh I see how you hide your pain
If it were only that easy to take it away
It doesn't matter if I give you the Earth
It doesn't matter when you love her

And you wonder why you want to stay
wild-eyed
Staying up and talking to me all night
Yet again, how my face could be anyone's
Yet again

It's ok to close your eyes
Sleep carries you away
Cradle your head in my arms
Hold you until you feel safe
The words that you speak weave a story
Just not the story you wanted to write
The tell-tales that I'm ignoring
Are keeping you up at night

Honey, what's the use?
Tell yourself the truth
Look it in the face
Before it takes you down

Always singing songs
Telling me I'm wrong
I can see I'm not
She still has your heart

Oh I see how you hide your pain
If it were only that easy to take it away
It doesn't matter if I give you the Earth
It doesn't matter when you love her.

17

I'm obsessed with everything that isn't me
Disinterested
I've told you so many times that I should be
alone
Yet you're surprised when I
Let you down
My mind goes to wild places
Cant you see that I'm insane?
You seem surprised when it rears its head. All
you want is a steady normality
With the sexy side of non conformity
What did you expect?
Attention and sex?
Silver linings made with extra spikes
My sanity isn't your sacrifice to make
My prescription isn't yours to take
My body's mine to abuse
How am I not telling the truth?
There's a difference between lying and selective
hearing
Never see my badness even when it's kicking
and screaming
Oh there's a little girl trapped inside
She's gonna bite.
There are thunderstorms in my head

The lightning strikes you down in bed
The electricity
Is flowing out from me
Don't be shocked if you get caught up
Girl you're too good to be the one they marry
Nobody will ever love them
Love them as hard as you can.
You're worth more than a ring and a pack of lies.
Give me a call and a pack of cigarettes any time
She danced with your boyfriend, singing
About blue and red
She promised it wouldn't go far
He was frightened you'd find out the things that
he said
But you were fucking his mate in the car.

18

The yellow left when the smoke has gone
He said he'd keep me safe from you
He didn't say it with words
He laid his lips over mine
Laid his body like a curse.

19

In recent times
I've found peace in the arms
Of water.

Close my eyes and watch the steam
At the same time
What if everything were as it seemed?
Is that the dream?

There is more than one of us
Dancing in front of you
Reality is compromised.

All we ask now
Is open your eyes

Open
Your
Eyes

20

It's not knowing when you're going to go from happy and smiling to wanting to smash a glass and slit your arms open.

It's wanting to be open and honest about some of the stuff in your head, but it's too big and too scary. You don't want to be scary. You don't want to be crazy.

It's about the fine like between the glamourised world of mental illness, where you're allowed a diagnosis as it makes you "edgy", but the moment you show any real symptoms you become a pariah. People leave you- people who said they would always love you, always be there, people who say they stand tall on behalf of mental health etc.
They will be the people that turn their backs. And why wouldn't they?
This has made you a true master of pushing people away- why wouldn't they walk away? Sometimes your behaviour can be utterly shocking, so that years later- even if you've overcome so much- people still judge you, avoid you, laugh at you behind your back. Why is it

funny to laugh at someone who's struggling with mental health issues? Beats me.

It's spending the majority of your life begging the system for help and support, but because you lurch from one job to another you're not unwell enough for support- you're "working".

It's doctors trying to plug the hole with drugs that aren't quite right and make it worse, that make you sleep all the time, that stop you sleeping at all, that make you feel like a robot, that make your brain feel like it's being electrocuted. Drugs that make you physically sick, and being you're "too complex" for counselling when in reality, mental health services are just so stretched that there aren't enough appointments.

It's a day off sick with a "tummy bug"- aka laying in bed, curled in a ball, shaking with terror and hardly breathing.

It's a day off sick with a "migraine"- aka numb, empty, using every bit of energy you can not to make today the day you finally do it.

It's a trip to the hospital for something other than "I tried, I failed. Of course I failed."

It's your family going on holiday with your brothers, sisters, their partner's.. but not you. You had a mental break once on holiday and they sent you home on the next flight.

It's not being a godparent to your nephews and nieces because your family think you're "crazy".

It's being scared to be open and honest with your partner because all they want is for you to be fixed and normal, and no matter how hard you work, sometimes that seems impossible.

It's self sabotage. It's building a life and fighting against something deep within yourself, a slow process, baby steps until one day you realise you don't want to end it all, you don't want to tear it all apart, you've achieved something. Only to be back at square one a week later.

It's the fear that your colleagues, friends, family will one day find out the truth about what goes on inside your head.

It isn't a happy ending sort of thing.

It isn't poetic.

It's my frustration over how backwards things really are in terms of mental health and the stigma surrounding it.

www.ingramcontent.com/pod-product-compliance
Lightning Source LLC
Chambersburg PA
CBHW051753130826
49812CB00033B/1137
* 9 7 8 9 3 5 7 4 4 3 3 1 9 *